MASTER SOLOS
INTERMEDIATE
LEVEL

**Edited & Performed
by Gary Sigurdson**

Flute

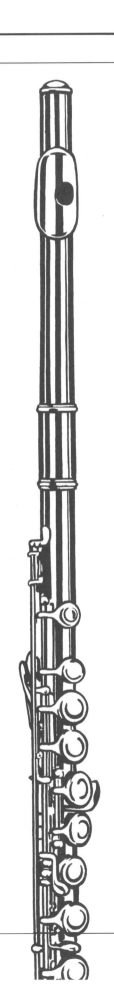

HAL•LEONARD®

Piano (Flute)   Intermediate Level

MASTER SOLOS
by Gary Sigurdson
Edited by Linda Rutherford

Contents

ISBN 978-0-7935-9544-0

HAL•LEONARD®

Copyright © 1976 by HAL LEONARD LLC
International Copyright Secured All Rights Reserved

No part of this publication may be reproduced in any form or by
any means without the prior written permission of the Publisher.

Visit Hal Leonard Online at
www.halleonard.com

Contact us:
Hal Leonard
7777 West Bluemound Road
Milwaukee, WI 53213
Email: info@halleonard.com

In Europe, contact:
Hal Leonard Europe Limited
42 Wigmore Street
Marylebone, London, W1U 2RN
Email: info@halleonardeurope.com

In Australia, contact:
Hal Leonard Australia Pty. Ltd.
4 Lentara Court
Cheltenham, Victoria, 3192 Australia
Email: info@halleonard.com.au

Entr'acte

Georges Bizet
(1838-1875)

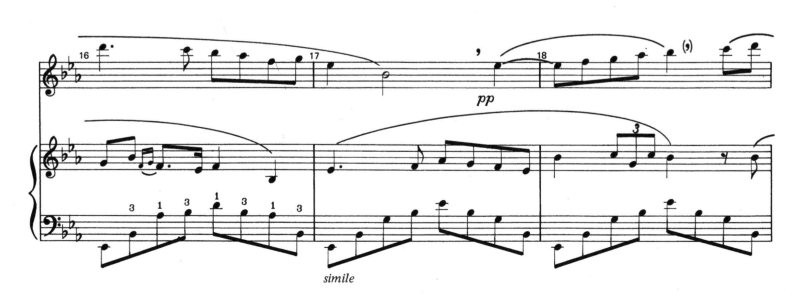

5

6

Menuet and Dance of the Blessed Spirits

Christoph Gluck
(1714 - 1787)

Spirit Dance

Largo and Allegro

Georg Ph. Telemann
(1681-1767)

Allegro

(M.M. ♩ = 114)

Andante

Wolfgang Mozart
(1756-1791)

(M.M. ♩ = 56)
Andante ma non troppo

Allegretto

Benjamin Godard
(1849-1895)

29

Passacaglia

Vaclav Nelhybel

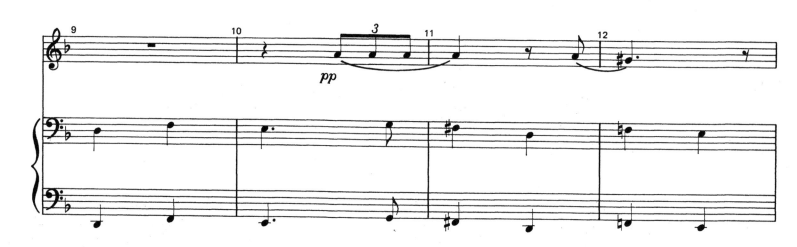

34

Scherzo

Vaclav Nelhybel

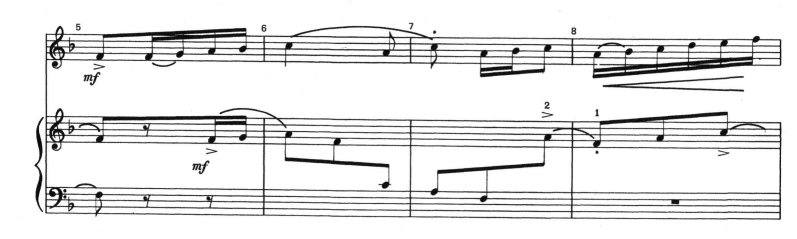

37

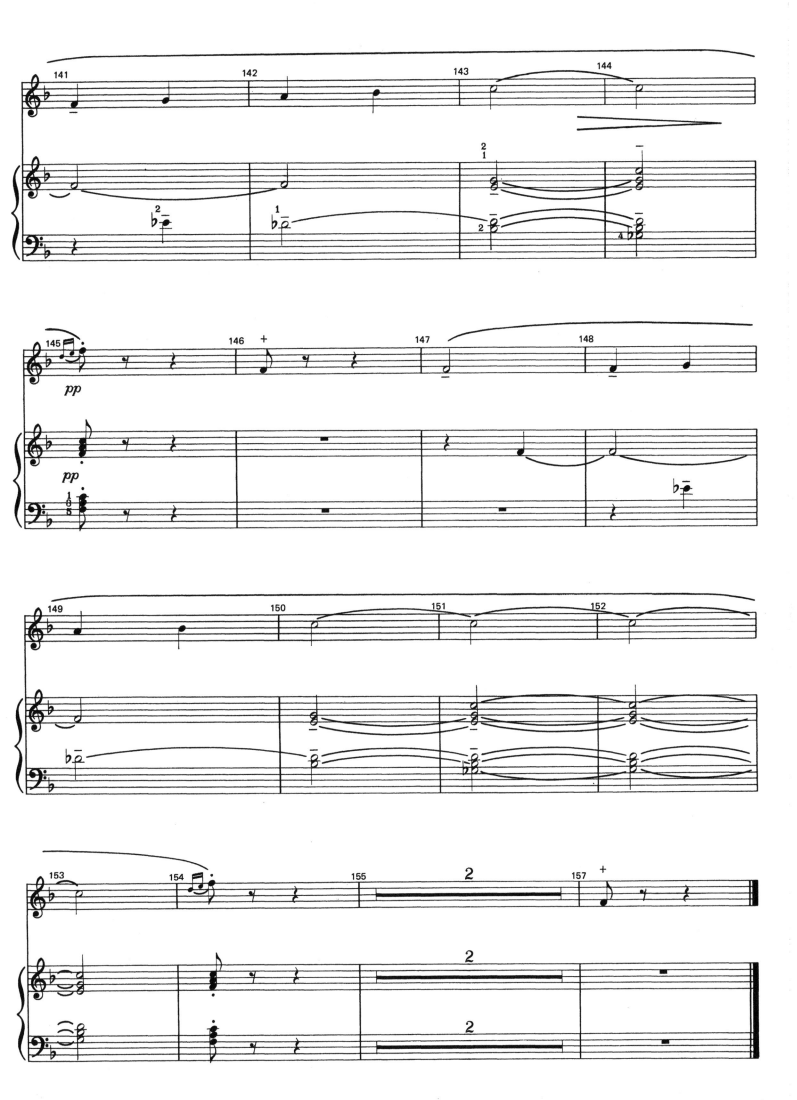

Carnival of Venice

Giulio Briccialdi
(1818-1881)

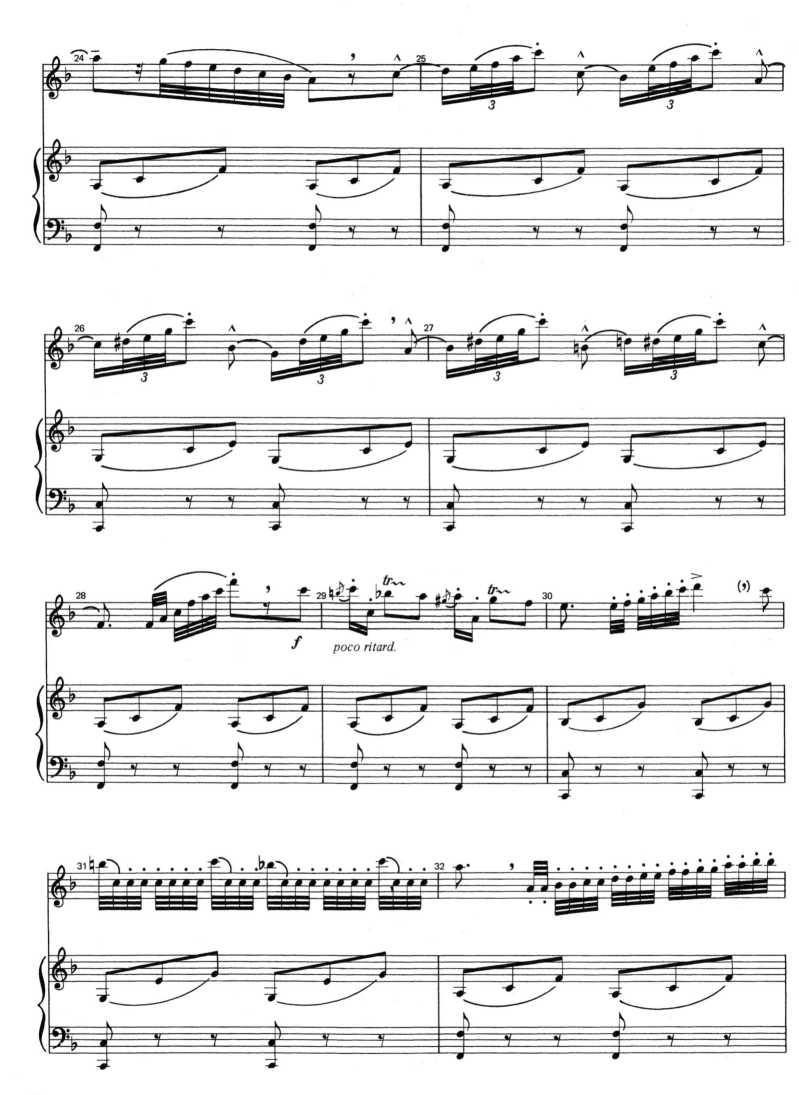

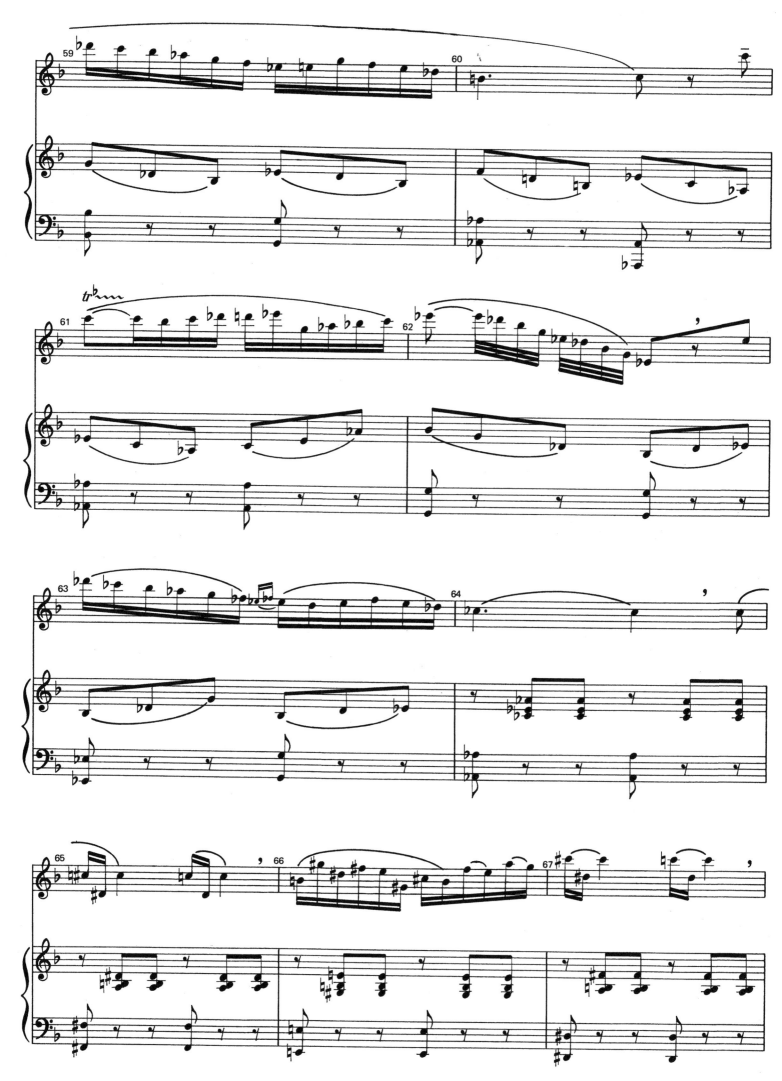